ELIJAH

INNER FIRE | OUTWARD ZEAL

The 2019 Lay Carmelite Convocation

of the
North American Province of St. Elias
and the
Province of the Most Pure Heart of Mary

CARMELITE MEDIA

Layout and Cover design by William J. Harry, O. Carm.

Printed Book ISBN: 978-1-936742-24-0

Ebook ISBN: 978-1-936742-25-7

CARMELITE MEDIA

1317 Frontage Road
Darien, Illinois 60561 USA

Phone +1-630-971-0724
Email: publications@carmelnet.org
Website: carmelites.info/publications

TABLE OF CONTENTS

+   +   +

(l-r) Rose Mary Lancellotti, T. O. Carm., and Cindy A. Perazzo, T. O. Carm., Provincial Coordinators for Lay Carmelites.

The 2019 Lay Carmelite Convocation was planned by the Interprovincial Lay Carmelite Commission of the St. Elias Province and the Province of the Most Pure Heart of Mary:

> Cheryl Baltru (PCM)
>
> Desi Byerley (PCM)
>
> Sr. Libby Dahlstrom (PCM)
>
> Rose Mary Lancellotti (SEL)
>
> Carol Marmo (SEL)
>
> Edith Matlock (SEL)
>
> Margie McCalester (PCM)
>
> Cindy Perazzo (PCM)
>
> Kathleen Richardville (PCM)

PREFACE

Gathering hundreds of Lay Carmelites every four years is a long-held tradition for the Provinces of the Most Pure Heart of Mary and St. Elias. The work of pulling a program together, choosing a theme and speakers and implementing a plan usually take years of coordination and planning. It is labor well spent, however, with the labor taken up by the Interprovincial Lay Carmelite Commission.

The theme for the 2019 Convocation held at the downtown Chicago Hilton, Illinois was *Elijah: Inner Fire-Outward Zeal* with the objective of displaying our inner life of prayer and how it translates into an outer life of ministry.

Lay Carmelites arrived from all corners of Canada and the United States for the event. Directors, Formation Directors, Regional Coordinators, and Regional Formation Coordinators arrived early for a program prepared to enrich their leadership ministry with Lay Carmelite communities. Old friends were greeted, and new friends made for a lifetime of collaboration and support in the Carmelite Way of Life.

We hope you enjoy this publication, which strives to present the featured speakers' reflections to assist all Lay Carmelites in his or her vocation.

The Interprovincial Lay Carmelite Commission is already working towards our next Convocation which we pray you will attend.

Cindy A. Perazzo, T. O. Carm.
Provincial Coordinator for Lay Carmelites, PCM

Rose Mary Lancellotti, T. O. Carm.
Provincial Coordinator for Lay Carmelites, SEL

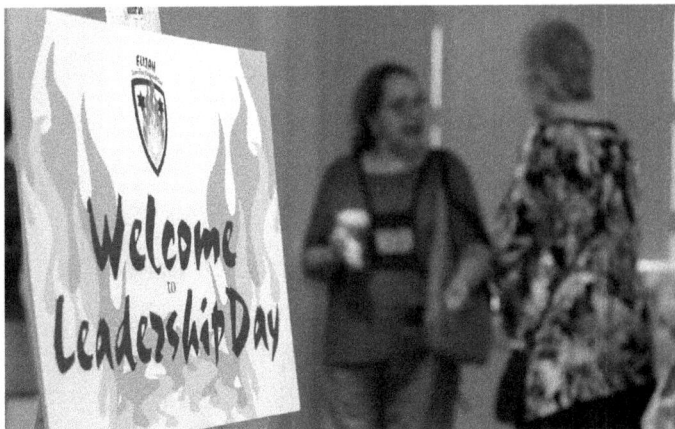

CONVOCATION SCHEDULE

FRIDAY, JULY 19

Noon - Registration begins

2 p.m. - Bookstore Opens

7 p.m. Welcome, Introduction, Evening Prayer

7:45 p.m. - **Keynote Address**
Blessed Titus Brandsma & Elijah:
Prophetism in Carmel
Fernando Millán Romeral, O. Carm.

9:00 p.m. - Social

SATURDAY, JULY 20

8:30 a.m. - Morning Prayer
9:00 a.m. - **Inner Fire**
Nicholas Blackwell, O. Carm.

9:45 a.m.- Break

10:15 a.m. - **Outward Zeal**
Glenn Snow, O. Carm.

11:00 a.m. - Break

11:45 a.m. - Celebration of Eucharist

1:00 p.m. - Luncheon

3:00 p.m. - Workshops start

INNER FIRE

Team #1 - Beth Fitzpatrick, O. Carm., Pat Molnar, T. O. Carm.
Team #2 - Desi Byerley, T. O. Carm., Kathleen Richardville, T. O. Carm.

OUTWARD ZEAL

Team #1 - Suki Carder, T. O. Carm., Albania Almonte, T. O. Carm.
Team #2 - Enidia Seoane,T. O. Carm., Carol Marmo, T. O. Carm.

4:00 p.m. - Break

4:30 p.m. - Workshops continue

5:30 p.m. - Break

6:00 p.m. - Evening Prayer

FREE EVENING

SUNDAY, JULY 21

8:30 a.m. - Morning Prayer

9:00 a.m. - **The Call of Elijah is Our Call**
William J. Harry, O. Carm.

9:45 a.m.- Break - Hotel Checkout Before Mass

11:00 a.m. - Celebration of Eucharist and Closing

CONVOCATION SPEAKERS

Albania Almonte, T. O. Carm.
Formation Director, Orlando FL (PCM)

. . .

Reverend Nicholas Blackwell, O. Carm.
St. Elias Province (SEL)

. . .

Desi Byerly, T. O. Carm.
Interprovincial Commission Member (PCM)

. . .

Suki Carder, T. O. Carm.
Director, Orlando FL (PCM)

. . .

Sr. Beth Fitzpatrick, O. Carm.
Sister of Mount Carmel, LA (PCM)

. . .

Very Reverend William J. Harry, O. Carm.
Prior Provincial, Most Pure Heart of Mary Province

. . .

Carol Marmo, T. O. Carm.
Interprovincial Commission Member (SEL). . .

. . .

Most Reverend Fernando Millán Romeral, O. Carm.
Prior General of the Carmelite Order

. . .

Pat Molnar, T. O. Carm.
St. Elias Province (SEL)

. . .

Kathleen Richardville, T. O. Carm.
Interprovincial Commission Member (PCM)

. . .

Enidia Seoane, T. O. Carm.
St. Elias Province (SEL)

. . .

Reverend Glenn Snow, O. Carm.
Most Pure Heart of Mary Province

. . .

The Prophet Elijah– This statue was created by Louis Laumen (https://www.louislaumen.com/) for the Golden Anniversary of Whitefriars College in Melbourne, Australia in 2010. The statue stands at the entrance to the school chapel while the nearby Reflective Garden contains a sculpture of Mary and the adolescent Jesus, capturing the two major inspirations of Carmelite spirituality. *(Photo courtesy of Whitefriars College, Melbourne)*

Fernando Millán Romeral, O. Carm.

Fr. Fernando is a native of Madrid, Spain and a member of the Baetica Province in the southern part of Spain. He studied at the Colegio Santa María del Carmen de Madrid. He studied philosophy at the Universidad Pontificia Comillas in Madrid and theology in C.E.T. in Sevilla, Milltown Institute for Philosophy and Theology in Dublin, and Comillas. In 1997 he received his doctoral degree from Pontifical Gregorian University in Rome. His thesis was on Carmelite Servant of God Bartholomew Xiberta's theology of sacramental reconciliation.

Fr. Fernando was ordained in 1989 in Madrid. He then began teaching at various schools, including as ordinary professor of Sacraments at Comillas. He has also taught as invited professor at the Pontifical Gregorian University. He has been a member of the Institutum Carmelitanum in Rome and the Centro de Estudios judeo-cristianos in Madrid and the International Commission for Culture of the Order. He is part of the editorial teams the magazines *Escapulario del Carmen*, *Sal Terrae*, *Fonte* and *Estudios Eclesiásticos*. He has been awarded various literary prizes.

He was elected prior general of the Carmelite Order in the 2007 General Chapter and was re-elected in 2013. He now resides in Madrid and teaches at Universidad Pontificia Comillas and is much sought after as a speaker.

BLESSED TITUS BRANDSMA AND ELIJAH:

PROPHETISM IN CARMEL

presented by Fernando Millán Romeral, O. Carm

To start I want to thank the organizers of this gathering for their very kind invitation to participate. This is the third time I have participated in these Lay Convocations. The first time was also here in Chicago, the second was in Atlanta, and here we are again in Chicago. They have each been very enjoyable gatherings, an opportunity to share our Carmelite spirituality and also our fraternity. Many thanks!

The theme chosen for our meeting this year is that of prophetism. Years ago, I was in Ireland, participating in a provincial chapter and from there I had to come to the United States to participate in a congress on St. Teresa on the occasion of the 500th anniversary of her birth. I showed the program of the US Congress to a Carmelite brother who, looked it over. He then said to me "Oh you are speaking before the experts..." Here again I find myself in the same situation. It is for me to speak first, before those who really know this topic!

Regardless I wish to share with you some brief reflections regarding the person of Blessed Titus Brandsma who has been compared— not without reason— as a new Elijah, a prophet for our time.

I am convinced that the life story, doctrine, and witness as a martyr of Fr. Titus Brandsma, is a true prophetic sign for Carmel in the 21st century and that his life inspires us to be— in circumstances very different than his but just as in need of hope and of meaning— true Carmelite prophets for men and women of our time.

ELIJAH IS IMPORTANT TODAY

I will begin this first point with something very obvious: the Prophet Elijah is an important figure for our time. To demonstrate this, I will briefly focus on three facts:

A) The great psychologist Carl Gustav Jung wrote that Elijah is one of the archetypes by which the collective unconscious of the Western culture is expressed. Elijah is, furthermore, a living archetype. Traditions are continually being generated which connect to his "essential archetype." The "essential" dominates the "constellated archetype" around the figure of Elijah as the various traditions are articulated, as stars in a constellation. We cannot spend much time on this point, but let me say that in a letter of the famous Swiss psychologist to the Discalced Carmelite psychologist Bruno de Jésus-Marie (who had written to Jung asking him about the process of formation of the archetypes), spoke of Elijah as one of the most significant archetypes with a series of characteristics that define him. Elijah, as with all essential or constellated archetypes, is presented under various forms and appearances. With an enormous understanding of the topic, Jung enumerates a list of literary, religious, and historical figures, which— in one way or another— emerge, become present, and take the form of this archetype.

In this sense, I dare to suggest two figures (two characters) who I consider as a modern day version of this archetype without pretending (I would be reckless to do so) to add to the impressive list of this great psychologist. The first would be the gypsy Arquímedes, from the novel *Cien años de soledad* (*One Hundred Years of Solitude*) by the Nobel prize winner Colombian author Gabriel García Márquez. In the mythical city of Macondo, there is the illness of insomnia that causes the loss of memories, of memory, and, finally, one's own identity ("*The consciousness of one's own being*"). Only upon the return of the old wise Melquíades does memory return. Melquíades comes to be one of these prophets, wise men, who reminds the town who it is and what is its mission.

The second example would be the celebrated Gandalf in the novel *The Lord of the Rings*. In him, as in Arquímedes, a series of characteristics are noted that remind us of Elijah: he is a holy knight with the values of goodness, nobleness, beauty, and justice; he faces the forces of evil; he does not die but disappears (in the caves of Moria); he returned to appear when the people are in most need; his memory and the hope of his coming survive.

B) Carmel has always reverently upheld the Prophet Elijah as an inspiration, patriarch, model, father, and guide (*Pater et Dux*) and even as founder of the Order. Certainly, there has been in this significant medieval legend (some of them genuinely enjoyable), baroque exaggeration (think of the statue by Cornacchini in St. Peter's Basilica in Rome) and of literary invention. However, we can not disparage the Carmelite devotion to the prophet just because of these. This devotion has inspired, in various periods of time and under various prisms, a rich spirituality and has helped to live in very different contexts, our Carmelite identity at the service of the Church and of humanity. It is enough just to recall the rich reflection the figure of Elijah generated in the worldwide Carmel regarding justice and peace following the Second Vatican Council.

Along this same line (the importance of Elijah, including today) I wish to highlight that two of the greatest Carmelites of our time, St. Teresa Benedict of the Cross and Blessed Titus Brandsma, have underlined the bonding of Carmel with the figure of Elijah. Edith Stein, Jew (and, therefore, familiar with certain Elian traditions), renowned philosopher, Carmelite nun, in a text in which she tries to explain her vocation to Carmel (*On the History and Spirit of Carmel*) and what that means, points out the following:

> What does the average Catholic know about Carmel? That it is a very strict, perhaps the strictest penitential Order, and that from it comes the holy habit of the Mother of God, the brown scapular, which unites many of the faithful in the world to us. The whole church celebrates with us the patronal feast of our Order, the feast of the scapular, on July 16. Most people also recognize at least the

names of "little" Thérèse and "great" Teresa, whom we call our Holy Mother. She is generally seen as the founder of the Discalced Carmelites. The person who is a little more familiar with the history of the church and monasteries certainly knows that we revere the prophet Elijah as our leader and father. But people consider this a "legend" that does not mean very much. We who live in Carmel and who daily call on our Holy Father Elijah in prayer know that for us he is not a shadowy figure out of the dim past. His spirit is active among us in a vital tradition and determines how we live. Our Holy Mother (Teresa) strenuously denied that she was founding a new Order. She wanted nothing except to reawaken the original spirit of the old Rule.

And Titus Brandsma himself, who I will speak of next, in the talks that he gave in the United States and Canada in his famous 1935 trip, pointed out the following:

> As in daily life, so also in spiritual life, it is of the greatest importance to have a model of inspiration, an exemplar for imitation. Carmelite spirituality has such a model (...). Here Israel heard his challenge in words of flame, as a burning torch. But here he was more than the Prophet of the sword, here he was also the first of a long line of those who would worship God in spirit and in truth."

Therefore, it seems clear that for these two figures of Carmel in the 20th century, Elijah is not a distant memory, not some infantile legend, but a living source and rich in inspiration for Carmel in our time. Our Constitutions of 1995 indicated this when they affirmed:

> From Elijah, Carmelites learn to be people of the

desert, with heart undivided, standing before God and entirely dedicated to his service, uncompromising in the choice to serve God's cause, aflame with a passionate love for God. Like Elijah, they believe in God and allow themselves to be led by the Spirit and by the Word that has taken root in their hearts, in order to bear witness to the divine presence in the world, allowing God to be truly God in their lives. Finally, in Elijah they see, not only prophetic wisdom, but also brotherhood lived in community; and with Elijah they learn to be channels of God's tender love for the poor and the humble." (Constitutions, 26)

C) The three great monotheistic religions all venerate to some extent the figure of the Prophet Elijah, maybe for the fact that, and from his name itself (*Eliyahu*, which usually is translated as "Yahweh is God" or "Yahweh is the Lord"), reminds us of the uniqueness and all powerfulness of God. In each of the three great monotheistic traditions (including inside each one of them) they stress different aspects and dimensions of the life and of the witness of the prophet.

In Judaism, this presence is very strong and meaningful. For example, in many synagogues you find the seat of Elijah, related to the circumcision. The Jews place this solemn chair in the ceremony of the circumcision for Elijah who comes to witness. He is also present in the Passover dinner (Seder meal) as well as — in some traditions— in the Sabbat. The fountain of Elijah in the Wadi es-Siah, is visited by rabbis who make ritual baths and ablutions. Elijah has in Judaism a double mission: recall and revive the covenant and prepare the way for the Messiah.

What is more, the Jewish tradition conserves the

beautiful *hadadot* about Elijah and his feats, collected in the Talmud. Also in the ambit of Judaism, come forth beautiful legends and histories about Elijah with a moralizing value.

In Islam, Elijah is the "always alive" (as he is called in the Koran), the "always green," the "leafy one." In the sentiment he is related to fertility and life. In some traditions this relationship is captured with the coming of the rain (following the text of I Kings 18), others underline that he celebrates Ramadan in Jerusalem and from there is taken to Mecca in a hidden way and in others he becomes manifest in his struggle against the idolatry of those from Baal.

Also in Christianity, the importance of Elijah is very large. Although it is a fact in an anecdotal way (which depends on the order in which the books of the bible are placed), it is still curious that the final two verses of the Old Testament (of the First Testament, as we who are involved in the Judeo-Christian dialogue prefer to call it) makes reference to Elijah:

> See, I will send the prophet Elijah to you before that great and dreadful day of the Lord comes. He will turn the hearts of the parents to their children, and the hearts of the children to their parents; or else I will come and strike the land with total destruction." (Malachy 4, 5-6)

We could almost say that those two verses situate Elijah as the hinge of both Testaments, as one who prepares us and disposes us for the Day of the Lord. Furthermore, John the Baptist (the precursor) is identified with Elijah and Christ himself as well.

Subsequently Christianity has highlighted Elijah's fight against idolatry, as well as his being the "founder" of the school of the *sons* of the prophets, the proto-prophet that, in some ways, inspired the basic attitudes of later propheticsm. In fact, the Eastern Christians, on the day of his feast (July 20) and on other days, celebrate him also as the "cornerstone of the prophets, the Most Holy Elijah" and he is acclaimed with songs. Likewise, Elijah was honored as a model of monasticism and the eremetical life. He is the solitary figure who is confronted with the mystery of God in difficult times. In this sense, the Carmelites have been the primary promoters of this devotion and admiration for the figure of Elijah, though not the only ones. In other eremetical traditions as well, he is venerated in much the same way.

It remains clear that the Prophet Elijah is a polyhedric figure, rich, fertile, provocative, and inspirational for a believer of our time. Elijah is a strong figure, identified with fire, with a sword, with the protection of the one, true God. He always lives in uncertain and difficult times, when all appears to be lost. In this milieu, he valiantly rises in defense of goodness, for what is noble and just, for beauty and life. Elijah never dies, but is abducted into heaven. He disappears in order to return in order to appear (with a distinctive appearance, new, illuminated, yet familiar) when the faith of the people falters, when hope is lost, and discouragement spreads.

TITUS BRANDSMA SPEAKS TO US ABOUT ELIJAH

As indicated earlier, Professor Brandsma dedicated one of the conferences he gave in North America in 1935 to the figure of Elijah. In that lecture (following the inspiration of the *Institutio primorum Monacho-rum*), he highlighted, above all else, the idea of his "double spirit." Here he stressed the importance of the connection the united the first Carmelites to the memory of Elijah. Brandsma signals that they are the heirs of his "double spirit." To what is he referring? The expression, according to the Dutch Carmelite, has a triple meaning:

A) The double portion of the inheritance in some traditions is for the oldest son (that is, two third of the inheritance) as is reflected in the celebrated Book of Kings in which Eliseus, successor of Elijah, asks for two-thirds of his spirit. (2Kgs 2: 9-10). However, Brandsma points out, that in order to receive this inheritance, we must be make ourselves worthy, to respond to that which the first born hopes for and to bring to completion the mission that corresponds to him:

> But only he who has the intention of maintaining the noble traditions of the house may ask this privileged portion. If we ask his double spirit in this sense, we have to be his first sons and to follow him as well as possible.

B) A second meaning of "double spirit" refers to how Elijah knew how to combine and harmonize the contemplative spirit (the man of prayer, the solitary figure who discovers the presence of God in the gentle breeze, the inspiration of the hermits) and the active spirit (the preacher, struggling against idolatry, the prophecies, etc) It is a terminology that perhaps today, in this sense, is a bit out of date (since it tends to point out that we all must be, in some way, contemplatives and actives; however it has certainly been important in Carmlite spirituality for centuries.

C) Finally, Brandsma stresses that the "double portion" is referring to

> the harmonious union of the human exercise of virtue and the divine infusion of mystical life; the union of the 'via purgativa' and 'illuminativa' with the '*via unitiva*'...

In Carmelite spirituality, therefore, a peculiar form was lived with this union between the the gift, grace (the infusion of the mystical life) and the commitment, the human response to the gift (the human exercise of virtue). Today we would say (using a frequently used word play in German theology) that the "double spirit" of Elijah reminds us that the spiritual life is *Gabe und Aufgabe*, or as we would say in English "gift and work." Brandsma himself made it even more precise affirming:

> It must be the union of active and passive contemplation, the union of human endeavor and the infusion of the mystical life by God. Our sufferings and sacrifices, our labors and exercises in prayer and virtue will be rewarded by God with the beatifying vision of His love and greatness.

The text is not only important because of its reference to the terminology of a great tradition of Carmelite spirituality but that it points already to the same form of living this spirituality that our man had: involved in a thousand different things, committed to justice and the defense of the most vulnerable (he spoke of the "exercise of virtue in individual or social activity"), untiring apostle, university professor, etc., and, at the same time, a man of prayer and with a deep interior life. So it is no surprise that

Brandsma concluded this section recalling that the figure of Elijah constitutes the best example of the Carmelite life.

Later in his talk, the Frison Carmelite reviewed some of the characteristics of Elian spirituality that Carmel tried to live and pass on over the centuries and that are considered the fundamental elements of our charism: to live in the presence of God, love of solitude (which include as well a distancing from the world and the asceticism), a profound Eucharistic piety represented in the bread offered by the angel in the desert (1Kgs 19:1-8), and the harmonious balance between intellectual prayer and affective prayer, a topic that Professor Brandsma had already dealt with in other writings.

In this list of Elian traits that Carmel has tried to recreate, our Carmelite also included Marian devotion, which – following an ancient tradition, very well developed in Carmel – would be prefigured in the white cloud that Elijah and his servant see from Mount Carmel. (I Kings 18: 41-46).

As I have already pointed out on other occasions, the key to understanding the spiritual life of Blessed Titus is to read his studies of various spiritual figures, that is, to analyze his choice of the various authors he was to study. All study supposes a filtering, an emphasis of certain aspects that, for one reason or another, attract the attention of the student more. The ancient scholastics said that *quod recipitur, ad modum recipientis recipitur* ("what is received by something, is received according to the condition of the receiver"). In the case of Fr. Titus, this is more important, if it is possible, to know something about his inner world, since he was very frugal with words and very discreet when it came to his spiritual experiences. For this reason, indirectly, we can infer and come to understand something more about his own spirituality through the "reflections" of other figures in the history of mysticism that he studied.

In short, Blessed Titus Brandsma is convinced that the figure of Elijah, in all its richness and significance, has been and is deeply inspiring to Carmelite life, not only in past eras, but also for our modern times. As he did with other subjects, the Dutch Carmelite thought that a serious work of interpretation is needed so that this Elian spirit can be truly significant in a society as different and as complex as that of the first half of the 20th century. It was a period in Europe that, on the one hand, was achieving very high levels of technical, scientific, and philosophical development, but, on the other, was slipping dangerously towards barbarism and destruction. It is in this context, where our Carmelite would show himself, humbly but firmly, as a new Elijah.

TITUS BRANDSMA: AN ELIJAH FOR OUR TIME

The idea of considering Titus Brandsma as a "new Elijah" is not mine. It was already suggested by a predecessor of mine, Fr. Kilian Healy (whom I was not lucky enough to know personally), who was Prior General of our Order from 1959 to 1971. Fr. Healy wrote a book on Elijah entitled *The Prophet of Fire*, which he dedicated a part of to Fr. Titus. He offered some very interesting stories, such as, the fact that the contribution made by Professor Brandsma to the prestigious *Dictionnaire de Spiritualité*, was first assigned to Fr. John of the Cross Brenninger, a famous German Carmelite of the last century, well known for his *Directory* for novices. But Fr. Brenninger declined and suggested Fr. Tito as a possible author for the *Carmes* entry, pointing out that he was much more prepared and was the right person for the job.

In his book, Father Healy calls Father Titus Brandsma: "a new Elijah for our times." But in what sense can we identify Blessed Titus Brandsma, martyr to Nazism in the 20th century, with a prophet who lived nine centuries before Christ and whose history is lost among traditions and legends? To further complicate the subject, both figures–Titus and Elijah—are polyhedral, complex, rich in nuances, and with a great variety of elements and dimensions. However, I dare to suggest two aspects that synthesize the attitude of the authentic prophet and that would invite us to consider (with some freedom, but not without a foundational basis) Blessed Titus Brandsma as a "new Elijah" of our time.

A) Brandsma's Commitment Against Nazism:

One of the most often repeated and quoted phrases of Blessed Titus is the one that says: "He who wants to win the world for Christ must have the courage to come in conflict with it." To be sure, in the last years of his life, Brandsma heroically displayed that courage. In May 1940, the Netherlands had been invaded by Hitler's troops. Although at first the occupation government wanted to give an impression that things were normal and they had a certain respect for the

Dutch institutions, it quickly became apparent that this was only a facade. Little by little, the government put out oppressive norms against the Dutch people and especially against the Jews.

The confrontation with Professor Brandsma had come, however, long before. In his philosophy classes he had denounced the fallacies of race, nationalism, and warmongering that were at the basis of National Socialist thought. Shortly after the Nuremberg Laws were enacted in 1935, a group of university professors, liberal politicians, Protestants, Socialists, and two Catholics (Henri Poels and Titus Brandsma) wrote a small booklet against the treatment of the Jews in Germany.

In a few words, each of the authors gave their opinion about these discriminatory measures that they considered unfair and unthinkable in a "modern Europe" of which Germany was a prominent part. In his writing, Professor Brandsma went so far as to affirm that "what is being done against the Jews in Germany is an act of cowardice."

In this way, it would be very interesting to compare his speech as Rector Magnificent of the Catholic University of Nijmegen in 1932, entitled *The Notion of God* (*Godsbegrip*) and the patriotic speech delivered by Martin Heidegger a year later when he was appointed Rector from the University of Freiburg im Breisgau. In both there are not only two conceptions of what the university should be, but two conceptions of life and of the human being. In fact, several of Fr Titus's speeches were already archived in the Gestapo offices and some German newspapers or

Nazi sympathizers (*De Volksche Wacht*) harshly criticized this "dangerous little friar."

At a Mass, celebrated in Dokkum in July 1939, in memory of Saint Willibrord and Saint Boniface, the apostles of Friesland, the Frisian Carmelite made a direct criticism of a neo-paganism that condemns love as a weakness. Father Titus did not hesitate to link the paganism of King Radboud (who the two missionaries bravely faced) with the prevailing ideology of National Socialism.

The confrontation between Brandsma and Nazism intensified greatly when German troops invaded the Netherlands in May 1940. As we have already indicated, in the first months of the occupation, the Nazis raised vain hopes that the invading power would be very respectful of the Dutch people. It was not to be so. In a completely flat country, without natural shelters, with a laborious and peaceful people, it was difficult to think of an armed resistance.

The Germans were aware that the true resistance of the Dutch would be more intellectual and spiritual than military. For this reason, from the very beginning they set a clear objective: to leave those merely technical and bureaucratic tasks in the hands of the Dutch, in order to give an image of normality that would not aggrevate the people, but to then tightly control the media and education, which, little by little, would become the means to achieve the total "conversion" of Holland to National Socialism and its annexation into the Third Reich.

Although we cannot go further into this now, the resistance of the Frisian Carmelite to certain unjust laws was tenacious and courageous. For example, he refused to obey the rule that required the expulsion of Jewish children from Carmelite schools. He also opposed–along with Archbishop De Jong and the Dutch episcopate–that Catholic newspapers be forced to include the National Socialist propaganda.

To assure this would not happen, in the final days of December 1941 and the first days of 1942, Brandsma personally met with almost all the editors of Dutch Catholic newspapers and informed them that, if they were to publish the instructions of the occupation government, they would lose their status as a Catholic publication. Brandsma was well aware of how delicate and difficult the issue was and the sacrifice he was demanding from the editors (many of whom were laymen), but he was pleased and somewhat surprised by the very positive and heroic reaction he encountered in his meetings with them.

However, these efforts did not go unnoticed by the occupation authorities and, for this reason, he was arrested on January 19, 1942. After being subjected to interrogations by SS Hauptscharführer Hardegen (during which the prisoner Brandsma, remaining serene but firm, maintained his convictions, even knowing the consequences that this could have and that, in fact, did have). After going through various prisons and concentration camps, he died on July 26, 1942 in Dachau.

Brandsma has been described on several occasions as a "martyr of the freedom of expression." This is what Pope John Paul II called him in an address to a group of journalists in February 1986. He has also been defined as a "prophet" who defended the rights of the most persecuted and oppressed of his time, a defender of certain basic and fundamental human values that were being trampled on in that insane Europe.

The short essay he wrote in jail, at the request of Sergeant Hardegen, about why Dutch Catholics were against National Socialism is a real treasure. His attitude can be clearly considered "prophetic" in the deepest, noblest, and most beautiful sense of the word. I think it is not, therefore, an exaggeration (even putting aside my affection for him since he was a member of our Order), to consider our blessed Titus as a "new Elijah" who opposed the Baals (the Aryan race, the nation, violence) and the oppressors of the 20th century.

B. A Deep Interior Life

But Titus Brandsma was not a politician (although his attitude had repercussions that could be classified as such), nor an ideologue, nor – least of all – a radical fanatic who felt called to commit suicide in the process of defending his faith. His posture was always calm, courteous, and evangelical. In the prisons and camps through which he passed, he always maintained that attitude, to the extent that he asked for the guards to be remembered in prayer.

His writings about the reasons for the opposition of Dutch Catholics to National Socialism, which we alluded to earlier, ended with a beautiful blessing:

> God bless Holland! God bless Germany! May God grant that these two people stand again side by side

in full liberty and peace, in full recognition of His glory for the good of these two nations so closely related to one another.

In this way, Father Titus made the fundamental vocation of every Christian come true: to bless. Moreover, all his life (although we do not have time to present it here), the Frisian Carmelite worked generously and with no small amount of enthusiasm for reconciliation, for coming together, and for dialogue, which totally separates him from those who only moves by political motivation (no matter how noble it may be) or by an ideological radicalism.

The reason for all this must be sought in his inner strength, in his deep spirituality that did not always transcend, perhaps due to his intense activity, as well as a certain discretion about his own spiritual experiences. However, that intense life of prayer, gestated for years, was the one that encouraged him during his confrontation with an unjust and inhuman regime, it was the one that guided him in terms of the evangelical values that he defended, and it was the one that comforted and encouraged him in the last months of his life, in dramatic conditions.

Saint John Paul II captured it very well in his homily at the beatification Mass of our Carmelite, on November 3, 1985 in the Basilica of Saint Peter. I had the great fortune to participate in this when I was a young Carmelite student. After describing some heroic traits of Titus Brandsma's personality, the Polish Pope–very sensitive to issues related to the Jews and the World War he himself suffered– pointed out sharply: "Certainly, such heroism is not improvised. Father Titus matured it during the course of a lifetime ..."

Indeed, the Carmelite priest had dedicated part of his academic life and his pastoral life to living and sharing a deep spirituality that had its roots, on the one hand, in the Carmelite tradition (especially as found in Saint Teresa of Jesus) and, on the other hand, in the so-called Rhenish Flemish spirituality and in *Devotio moderna* (Modern Devotion).

This led him to delve further into various topics and aspects of the faith and Christian life, always with that balance (perhaps it is more accurate to say "that harmony") between being solidly anchored in tradition (something that he lived with passion) and a sincere and cordial openness to modern times, to the heartbeat of our society, to "the joys and the hopes, the griefs and the anxieties of the men of this age, especially those who are poor or in any way afflicted," to use the famous expression that, a few decades later, would begin the pastoral Constitution *Gaudium et Spes* of the Second Vatican Council.

There are many themes in which Titus Brandsma lived that synthesis between tradition and modernity. We cannot go further into this here, but what we are most interested in highlighting is that he lived them not only in a "professional" or academic way, but as something deeply assumed, something that resonated inside him, something so profound, it would be worth giving your life, if necessary.

One of those themes that I would like to mention is his piety for the passion of Jesus Christ expressed, above all, in Brandsma's comments regarding the *Via Crucis*. Indeed, throughout his life, Brandsma studied this piety in various ancient and modern authors. In addition, he himself wrote two commentaries on the Stations of the Cross in very different, but very curious circumstances.

The first was written on the occasion of the controversy that arose over the paintings of the Belgian expressionist Albert Servaes. At the request of a Discalced Carmelite, Jerónimo de la Madre de Dios, he had painted the Stations of the Cross in a very modern and somewhat surprising style for the times, which is why the series created puzzlement and scandal. Various European intellectuals such as Cardinal Désiré-Joseph Mercier, Jacques Maritain, Reginald Garrigou-Lagrange, and Laurentius Jansens, Abbot of Maredsous (who was one of the harshest critics of the work) all intervened in the controversy.

The controversy grew, eventually reaching Rome. The Holy Office prohibited the Servaes series from being exhibited in places of worship. At that moment, Fr. Brandsma intervened. He had tried earlier to mediate through the Procurator General of the Order in Rome, his friend Humbert Driessen but was unsuccessful. Brandsma advised Servaes and the Discalced Carmelite to obey the Order of the Holy Office, but–in one of those Solomonic decisions so typical of our Carmelite–he decided to reproduce the work in a newly founded magazine, *Opgang,* accompanied by a beautiful commentary for each station prepared by Brandsma himself.

The second *Via Crucis* that Titus Brandsma prepared, was done in more dramatic fashion. From a very young age, Brandsma had felt great sympathy and devotion for the Frisian apostles: Willibrord and Boniface. According to tradition, the latter had died in Dokkum, in the year 754, at the hands of the early Frisians who resisted evangelization. Father Titus had worked hard to have a chapel rebuilt in honor of Saint Boniface in Dokkum.

When it was inaugurated, he himself preached in several languages, including the Frisian of his native land. While in Scheveningen prison, he prepared a new commentary on the Stations of the Cross that surrounded this chapel in Dokkum. This is a much shorter commentary than the one done for Servaes but done with truly exceptional testimonial value. Professor Brandsma, Father Titus, the prisoner, thus joined himself to the Way of the Cross.

Perhaps the highest degree of piety for the Passion was reached by the Dutch Carmelite in his famous poem while in Scheveningen prison. With a mystical and sometimes heartbreaking tone, the prisoner unites himself with the pain of Christ and proclaims that, while Christ is by his side, he fears nothing and lacks nothing. It is not surprising that, from the moment the poem was made public, it has been reproduced, translated into different languages, recited or sung and, above all, that it has served as a comfort and a balm for so many people in situations of suffering or pain. The two *Via Crucis* and the poem *Before Jesus* are two of the best examples of the spiritual richness of Blessed Titus Brandsma.

We can conclude that Titus Brandsma, like every true prophet, was a mystic, a believer who had experienced the transforming presence of God in his life, a contemplative who, looking at the daily reality that surrounded him (even in most dramatic moments!) knew how to discover the small fragile signs of God's presence. Many of the witnesses declared this during the beatification process, from his brother Henry to Professor Christine Mohrmann, as well as several Carmelite brothers and the Dutch humorist Godfried Bomans. All of them asserted, in different ways, that Titus Brandsma lived passionately (without any kind of extravagant behavior) that presence of God in life that characterizes true mystics.

To highlight some testimonies that I consider very significant, I would just like to share with you three ideas extracted from the statements made by some Protestants who lived with Blessed Titus in the concentration camps. I think they are very beautiful and show that interior life visited and enriched by the grace of God that our Carmelite was shaping throughout his life. For example, Anne Sape Fogtelo, a Mennonite who was with Blessed Titus both in Scheveningen and later in Amersfoort, pointed out that Father Titus made a deep impression on her and adds: "One who acts like this in this type of an environment, must be a spiritually extraordinary man."

The second testimony corresponds to one of the Protestant pastors, Jack Overduin, who Brandsma encountered in the Dachau concentration camp. Overduin was invited later to testify in the beatification process. Overduin swore in his statement:

> Of what follows I can offer full assurance: all colleagues spoke with great esteem and respect for Titus Brandsma. His well-known poem reflects his full trust in God (...). I still remember finding him in

the bathroom a day or a few before his death. At that moment he knew his time was near. He was at peace and resigned to the situation.

The third testimony comes to us indirectly through Christine Mohrmann, first a student and later a colleague of Professor Brandsma. Professor Mohrmann, an expert in Latin philology, was not prone to sweeten up the figure of the Servant of God Brandsma in her statement. She was a woman with her own criteria and an ability to be quite critical. So her testimony becomes even more valuable. This teacher said that at a conference she met someone who had met with Fr. Titus at the Lager. He was a student of the Free Calvinist University of Amsterdam, who–when Professor Mohrmann told him that he had collaborated with Brandsma in Nijmegen–confessed that "he had only begun to believe in the existence of the saints when he met Titus Brandsma in captivity."

However, I would not want to end this presentation without mentioning that Titus was not a superman, nor a fanatic, nor a suicide bomber, not even a hero, if by "hero" we mean a person with special powers. He was a humble believer, a man of faith who also went through moments of fear, anguish, and even discouragement.

After the fruitful weeks that he spent in Scheveningen, where he carried out various works, in Amersfoort and later in Kleve, Fr. Titus passed through his dark night. He was feeling weaker and sicker. His strength was leaving him. Thus, after the success of his first conference to the other prisoners in Amersfoort (in which he spoke of Gert Grote) on Good Friday in 1942, he gave a second talk a few days later.

Witnesses say that the words did not come as quickly and he looked tired and dejected. Some of the prisoners who lived those difficult days with him even pointed out that he was sometimes disoriented and even crying. Titus Brandsma was also tempted to sit by the broom tree and invoke the Lord with those terrible words of the prophet: "Enough, Lord! Take my life, for I am worth no more than my ancestors" (I Kings 19: 4).

But this new Elijah also knew how to find his strength in the bread that some "angels" offered him. The few times in which he was able to receive communion with a particle of a consecrated host that was supplied to him by one of the imprisoned German priests or with a piece of consecrated host that he hid in the case for his glasses, Father Titus felt in his soul the words that Elijah heard in the desert: "Get up and eat, because the journey will be very long" (I Kings 19: 4). And with the little strength that he had left, but with a truly admirable trust in the Lord, he also knew how to head towards Horeb, the mountain of God which, in this case was also his Mount Calvary.

+　　+　　+

Inside Nijmegen's "Titus Brandsma Memorial," a collection of memorabilia, panels, personal belongings, etc, of Blessed Titus are preserved. Outside, in a kind of open circle serving as an entrance to the Memorial and surrounding the magnificent statue by Dutch artist Arie Trum, there is a wall on which are placed numerous plaques that commemorate the Carmelite communities around the world that have collaborated in the construction of this memorial. It is a beautiful sign of gratitude, of international fraternity, and of communion between all the branches of the Carmelite family.

That wall is presided over by the biblical phrase of the prophet Elijah that for centuries has been almost a Carmelite motto: *Zelo zelatus sum pro Domino Deo exercituum* (I Kings 19:14). May that zeal of Elijah that led Blessed Titus Brandsma to give courageous witness of the faith to its ultimate consequences, also move the Carmel of the 21st century, in a changing, complex, and fascinating world, to bear witness to God's love for all and especially for the weakest.

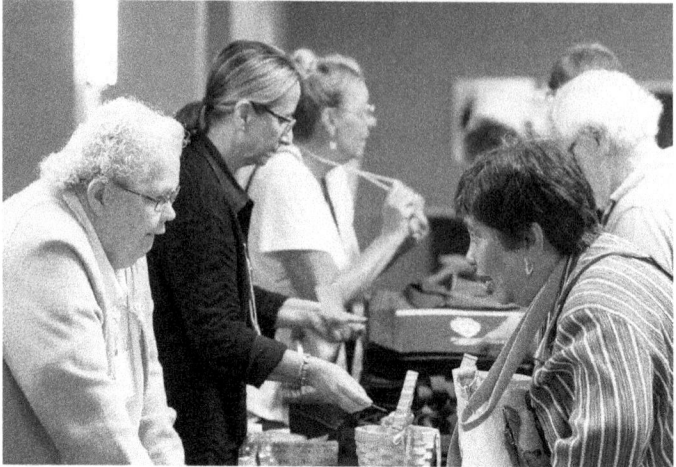

Staff of the Lay Carmelite Office receiving participants at the sign-in table. On the far left is Sr. Mary Martin, O. Carm., who retired as Provincial Coordinator for the Lay Carmelites (PCM) in 2017.

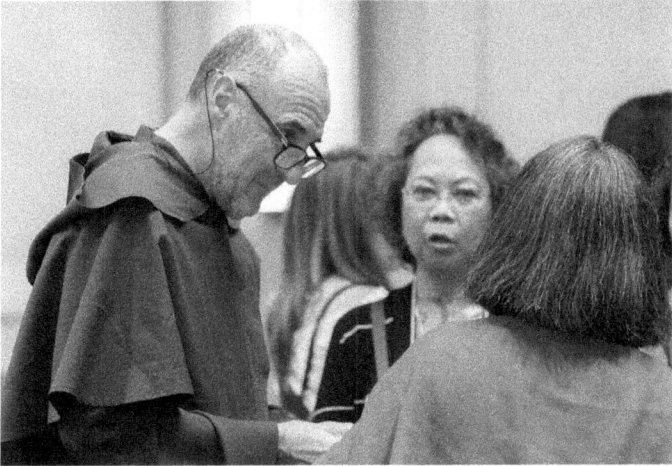

The Carmelite prior general, Fr. Fernando Millán Romeral, chatting with Lay Carmelite attendees.

Nicholas Blackwell, O. Carm.

Fr. Nicholas was born in Cass City, Michigan, and grew up in Mayville, Michigan in 1983. During his college years at Northern Michigan University, he got involved with the Catholic Campus Ministry group on campus and began discerning a vocation to religious life. After college, Fr. Nicholas spent a year in Gambia working with the Peace Corps. Upon returning he looked into a few other religious communities settling on the Carmelites, mainly because of their focus on community life and devotion to Our Lady of Mount Carmel and the brown scapular. He solemnly professed on July 16, 2016. Following ordination to the priesthood in August 2017, Fr. Nicholas was assigned as parochial vicar at St. Simon Stock-St. Joseph parish in the Bronx, New York. He is now assistant vocation director of the St. Elias Province and resides at Mount Carmel in Middletown, New York. He is responsible for the YouTube channel, The Frank Friar.

CARING FOR THE INNER ZEAL

presented by Nicholas Blackwell, O. Carm.

(Preface: This article is taken from the notes and structure that the original talk was given from during the Convocation.)

INTRODUCTION: CARMEL A TRUE PLACE FOR ZEAL

Fire, if not respected and cared for, has a way of becoming wild. A wildfire burns the good and the bad. This is not the type of fire we are meant for as followers of Jesus Christ. Our fire, what has been given to us, is a fire that that consumes but does not eviscerate, like the fiery bush made known to Moses. Therefore, as Carmelites we need a way; things to guide us in the care and cultivation of this inner flame of zeal that the Holy Spirit has enkindled in our hearts.

As Carmelites, we understand our rule of life calls us to a structured way of living that is rooted in a strong notion of place. Carmel is not merely an idea left to one's abstract modes of thinking, where one's desire for how things ought to be, is shaped. Carmel was and is a place rooted in a physical reality that we are called to emulate. The inner zeal is a driving force for that reality. Thus, from our local places of Carmel, we are called to emulate what existed in that place. It is in the formation of place that we see role for zeal as put before us in the Bible. Remember, the Bible is a library that makes known to us the need for a place of intimacy with God. It is from "a place" shaped by zealousness, given a foundational structure via studying and praying with the Bible that a tapestry of life is woven that makes known the splendor of Carmel lived in the world for God through his people.

PART ONE – INNER ZEAL: A GIFT OF AN ENCOUNTER

As mentioned, encounters always happen in a place. God comes to us where we are at. We may not know the moment when he chooses to encounter us in his own ways, but it is always where we are at. Thus, being a people attuned to the places that we are in, as Carmelites, is of the utmost importance, because the zeal poured forth into our hearts is always meant to impact the places where we are at.

Now, since I have used the term zeal several times, I think it is important to wrestle with that term. I like the word wrestle because it calls forth a means of physicality that is always necessary to the spiritual life. We, humans, are not merely corporal or spiritual, we are both, thus the term wrestling reminds us in this context that even though the inner zeal of a Carmelite is spiritual it is always lived in reality through our physical lives in the world. Now, zeal, as a divine gift, is an aspect of love, because it arises from an encounter with the one who is Love, God.

His presence impacts our hearts giving a birth to the spark of zeal for our hearts, his place of intimacy with us. This zeal, like a flame, gives us an energy and an enthusiasm to pursue the one we love. Zealousness is a noble passion. We zealously journey from, to and up Mount Carmel. A place where God has cultivated a place for ultimate nourishment expressed through the image of a vineyard.

Why Fire? This question highlights the symbol of fire as an important one for us to analyze to grow in reverence for the zealousness we are all called to. God's gifts always bring us forth from ignorance. Remember, the divine gift of fire is a means for illumination and, hence understanding. Now, fire calls for respect and care. Arrogance can cause us to fall like Icarus. The moment we do not respect fire and act imprudently it will burn us and others. The virtue of prudence is not an enemy to zeal but a profound companion for it. Prudence reminds us that the zealous fire is fragile and dangerous.

Seeing that this zealous fire calls for respect and care going forward I am going to refer to the fire triangle, something taught to me as a boy scout many years ago. There are three things all fire needs to exist: Heat, Oxygen, and Fuel. If anyone thing is lacking or in excess the fire dies or goes wild. Now, picture a triangle in your mind. The reaction of the three elements play a role in the birth zeal that resides in the middle of the triangle. The three aspects we need to care for the zeal given to us are:

    1) <u>Recollection</u>: The Heat that means by which the flames of love arise from in the heart.

    2) <u>Detachment</u>: The removal of barriers to allow

the air of the Holy Spirit to move within you.
3) Silence: The sacrificial fuel that feeds the fiery flames of love.

PART TWO – HEAT: THE NEED FOR RECOLLECTION

Recall, Elijah under the broom tree. His story is our story, so this moment of encounter with the divine is a gift that we can carry with us. As God goes to our Father Elijah, he does the same for us. For example, by recalling that moment in Elijah's life, we recall that God meets us where we are at to aid us and direct us to where we are called to be. A call he gives to us always in love. My big sister St. Teresa of Avila gives us two needed insights on recollection:

> "If you grow accustomed to having Him present at your side, and He sees that you do so with love and that you go about striving to please Him, you will not be able – as the say – to get away from Him; you will find Him everywhere. ~ *The Way of Perfection*

> "I tried as hard as I could to keep Jesus Christ, our God and Our Lord, present within me, and that was my way of prayer."

PART 3: DETACHMENT: REMOVING BARRIERS AND FEEDING THE ZEAL

As we shift to detachment, we begin to take the steps into the desert as our Father Elijah did. When we enter a place, like the desert, we only take what is necessary. All unnecessary things weigh us down and keep us from breathing in the air around us in the most harmonious way possible. The act of detachment opens a pathway for the flame of zeal, stocked via recollection, to receive the oxygen that it needs to live. In this case the oxygen that comes is the breeze of the Holy Spirit. In Carmel, St. John of the Cross gives us the following insight about detachment:

> Love consists not in feeling great things but in having great detachment and in suffering for the Beloved. (#115, Sayings of light and love)

> It is seriously wrong to have more regard for God's blessings than for God himself: prayer and detachment. (#138)

The danger arises from the affects that forge the bond of attachments! We must never forget loving and liking are not the same things for the Christian. The gifts from God, like consolations, can easily become what or who we see as God, thus leading us into idol formation. Via these false notions that we become attached to the inner flame of zeal becomes starved and our sight becomes limited. Here are some Biblical insights to aid us in our desire to become detached from the false gods we construct in our lives.

Detachment lends itself toward a spiritual freedom that we see expressed in St. Paul's 2 Cor. 3: 17 he writes "*Now the Lord is the Spirit, and where the Spirit of the Lord is, there is freedom.*" Like the winds that raise a bird into the air, so the Spirit does for those that are not bound to earthly things. Then there is Galatians 5:1, "*For freedom Christ set us free; so stand firm and do not submit again to the yoke of slavery.*" We are meant to be free in Christ, and we play an active role in the freedom he has won for us freely, thus working to free one's self from the idols in their life aids the growth of zeal when it is down in union with the Holy Spirit. Then there is 1 Peter 2:16 "*Be free, yet without using freedom as a pretext for evil, but as slaves of God.*" Freedom is not a license for a Christian. Freedom's end is union with Christ, who is the source of life itself.

This work of detachment is not merely about weeding the heart but as the Carmelite rule calls us too, we need to strive for a pure heart. As St. Matthew 5:8 reminds us "*Blessed are the clean of heart, for they will see God.*" Purity is not a mere cleanliness of the heart, even though that is a necessary aspect. Purity of heart is also about a focus. A pure heart is one that is focused on God. Sails require a sailor to be focused on the movement of the wind, so the heart must be focused in relationship to the movement of the Spirit. To support this notion, we also see Matthew an insight in 6:26 "*Look at the birds in the sky; they do not sow or reap, they gather nothing into barns, yet your heavenly Father feeds them. Are not you more important than they?*" The heart becomes focus when it worries not to fear about its own needs but learns to rely on the source of life, God. A pure heart strives for that freedom of faith in God. St. John writes also in 3: 18-20:

> "Children, let us love not in word or speech but in deed and truth. [Now] this is how we shall know that we belong to the truth and reassure our hearts before him in whatever our hearts condemn, for God is greater than our hearts and knows everything."

A free and pure heart has the ability move freely in itself from the Holy Spirit. By this movement, the Holy Spirit keeps our hearts from becoming stale and lifeless. Recalling our movement through a desert, detachment keeps the heart from becoming petrified, like a stone that sinks in the sand of the desert as it rolls across it. Elijah could move across the sand of the desert for 40 days because he was not weighed down but supported by the movement of the Holy Spirit in his heart.

PART FOUR – SILENCE: FUEL FOR THE FIRE & SACRIFICE OF TIME

Silence always requires time. Thus, moments of silence, like all prayer, is a sacrifice. When we sit in silence, we make a sacrifice of time which is an act of faith. We only have so much time so when we give it back to the Lord it is a testimony of trust, made in faith, that God is there in that moment and place with us. Silence is a way the gift of faith is opened and embraced. It was in silence that Elijah dwelt in the mountain. The world around him however was not silent, but he was able to dwell in silence. Silence is not a mere absence of sound, but a means of the heart to let go of its relationship with the noise of the world. St. Mary Magdalen de' Pazzi offers us some keen insights here, *"He is heard by all in His frequent utterance and in His profound silence." … "If you do not practice sweet silence it is impossible for you to taste the things of God!"* God speaks in the silence we strive to reside in because through silence we become attuned to God so we can perceive and receive his utterances.

There is nothing new here in these thoughts on silence. In Habakkuk 2: 20 we read *"But the LORD is in his holy temple; silence before him, all the earth!"* Via Habakkuk we can see God's sovereignty over the that of idolatrous tyrants of the earth. Our hearts are his temple where the fire of his love dwells, thus his presence makes it possible to perceive the adoration that creation gives over to its Creator. In this light, we are offered another vignette to see that silence is like a disposition of the heart by which we can penetrate the deeper reigns of existence around us. We also read in Psalm 62: 1, 5: "*For God alone my soul waits in silence; from him comes my salvation… For God alone my soul waits in silence for my hope is from him.*" Our lives that strive for silence is supported by patience, a virtue linked with courage, that is the habit of enduring current sufferings over time for a greater Good. Here is where hope allows us to sense God, who we rest in, even though his embrace comes across to us in the darkness of the night. To sit in silence patiently allows one's heart to grow in love through the darkness of the night. As Carmelites, through formation we learn that during the dark nights to trust in our beloved's hidden actions of love.

CLOSING

As the inner fire of zeal begins to grow in our hearts the tapestry of God's providence is slowly revealed to us in our moments of prayer with Him. God is the penultimate artist and the zealous eye that can focus on Him begins to see the beauty of his work that is unfolding in the world around themselves. Our sight grows through a zeal founded in faith. In faith the zealous eyes of our hearts grow in a trusting gaze that through the sacrifice time. Time that we just want to sit and be with a friend, our friend, God. Through patiently endure moments of darkness that arise from dwelling in silence hope makes it possible for the growth of the heart toward the world around it, like the pedals of a flower. In that beauty the eyes of our neighbors learn to see God. All of this is possible because the zealous flames offered the energy needed to enter the garden of God. A garden that is now the human heart where he has chosen for his seed of love to dwell. In his love the flames of zeal make it possible for the above actions in the garden to become animated and not relegated to mere ideas. Remember, these days (the convocation) are so important for the vocations we received. Why? They help to highlight the necessary things of life while also challenging us to go deeper into them through the gift of our minds. God never calls us to ignorance! I invite you now to spend time in your lives to consider, two biblical guides for us in the zeal we have received, *"His disciples remembered that it was written, 'Zeal for thy house will consume me.'"* (John 2: 17). Never forget all vocations arise from the love of God. A love that consumes us but does not annihilate us. Zeal resides in us but never come from us because it is a gifts meant to be carried for, nourished, and shared. The second item to consider is *"Brethren, my heart's desire and prayer to God for them is that they may be saved. I bear them witness that they have a zeal for God, but it is not enlightened."* (Romans 10:1-2). Zeal must never be isolated but treated as a flame entrusted to a home that is our heart. A home meant to receive guests, like the home of St. Martha.

Finally, our Order has given us the necessary tools to care for that flame that exists in our hearts.

1) Recollection: The Heat of love's flames arise

from it.

2) Detachment: Removes barriers to allow the air of the Holy Spirit to move in us freely.

3) Silence: The sacrificial fuel that feeds the flames of love.

I want to give the last words to St. Paul for this article *"Never flag in zeal, be aglow with the Spirit, serve the Lord."* ~ Romans 12:11

ELIJAH
[Inner Fire | Outward Zeal]

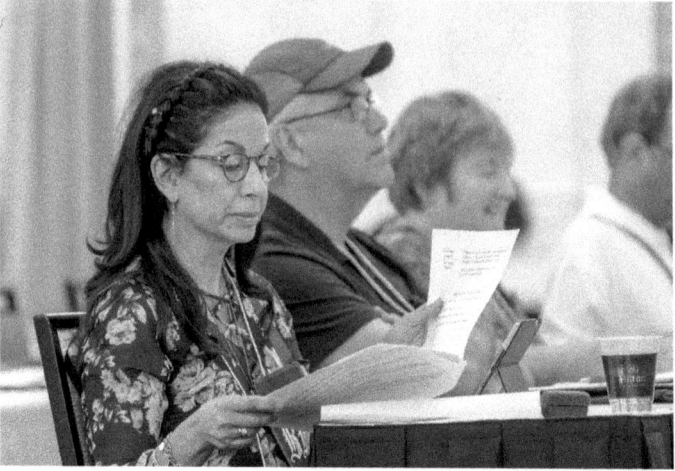

Lay Carmelite community leaders attending the one day training workshop prior to the start of the convocation.

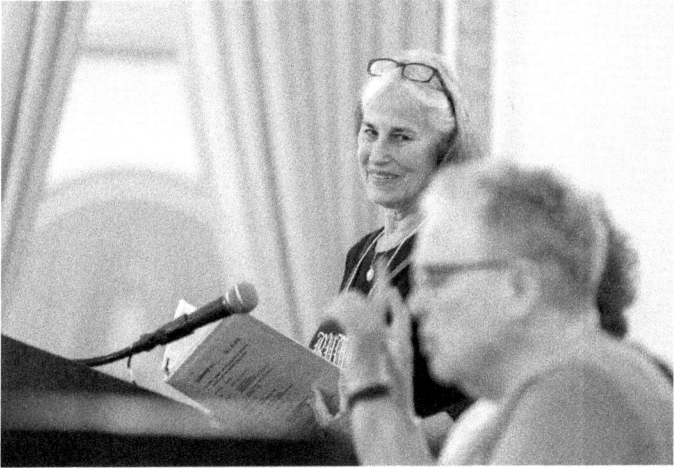

Inter-provincial Commission members Kathleen Richardville and Margie McCalester giving a presentation at Leadership Day.

Glenn Snow, O. Carm.

Fr. Glenn grew up in Southern California in the 60's and 70's. He earned a degree in history from California State University and Masters degrees in theology from the Washington Theological Union and in Negotiation and Dispute Resolution from Creighton University. As a Carmelite, Fr. Glenn has ministered for 20 years at several of the Carmelite high schools around the country in various positions. He also served at St. Cyril parish in Tucson, Arizona and St. Agnes parish in Phoenix, Arizona.

For a number of years, Fr. Glenn was part of the retreat team at the Carmelite Spiritual Center in Darien, Illinois. Since graduation from Creighton University, Fr. Glenn has also worked in Conflict Management which included workshops, interventions, and conflict coaching – where he helped people manage conflicts in families, dioceses, parishes, schools, convents, monasteries, nursing homes, and hospitals. He wrote the popular booklet on Carmelite history and the charism entitled *Foundation Stones* which is published in both English and Spanish. His love of history and road trips led him to become the historian of the ghost town of Gleeson, Arizona.

Fr. Glenn is currently serving as pastor of Immaculate Conception-St. Joseph parishes in Leavenworth, Kansas. He is also currently serving as an adjunct professor at Creighton University, teaching conflict management.

ELIJAH: OUTWARD ZEAL

presented by Glenn Snow, O. Carm.

Do you remember the Alfred Hitchcock movie "North by Northwest"? It starred Cary Grant, Eva Marie Saint, and James Mason, among others. Very near the end of the movie, there is a scene where little teeny Cary Grant is scrambling around the giant figures of Washington, Jefferson, Lincoln, and Teddy Roosevelt. That's how I felt a year and a half ago when I saw my name on the list of people they'd asked to speak this weekend. That guy there? That's Fernando Millan, Prior General of the Order. This other guy over there? That's Bill Harry, Prior Provincial of the PCM Province. But this guy who's standing at the podium right now? Oh I don't know, he's some associate pastor from Phoenix or somewhere. Just call me little tiny Cary Grant.

The topic that is my part in this convocation is "Outward Zeal". As Carmelites, our understanding of the word "zeal" comes from our scriptural interpretation of the story of Elijah. In particular, as he stood at the cave on Mount Horeb and spoke the words which are emblazoned on every generation of our Carmelite shield since the 1400's: *"Zelo Zelatus*

Sum Pro Domino Deo Exercituum." I am filled with a jealous zeal for God.

The context for this statement of Elijah's is that it is his response to the question posed to him by the Lord God. "Elijah, what are you doing here?"

One of the things that I do is teach conflict management for Creighton University. I have a Master's in Negotiation and Dispute Resolution from that same university, and nowadays I mostly teach nurses and medical students in their various graduate degree programs. I also do conflict coaching, which means that I meet with people (mostly pastors, associate pastors, deacons, sisters, and the occasional Carmelite), either individually or in small groups, to introduce them to some tools for dealing with conflicts in ways that work better for them than what they've tried before.

One of the tools I offer them is what I call "Messing with rhetorical questions."

Now we all remember what rhetorical questions are… we've gotten them from the time we were little kids. A mom speaking sternly to her little boy: "Do you think I'm stupid?!!?" You're NOT supposed to answer that question, kid! Your job is just to look down and shuffle your feet and mumble something. "Susie, so you think money grows on trees?" "Well, no, Mom… actually, the Federal Reserve Board, which is made up of distinct and semi-independent federal reserve banks, comes together…" Shhhh! Hey, little Warren Buffet! You're not supposed to answer rhetorical questions!

Rhetorical questions are posed in order to make a

point, not in order to get information.

So, one of the things I do in conflict situations is to mess a little with people's rhetorical questions. Sometimes it's helpful even to mess around a little with REAL questions, because you can create a different emphasis. That's what I'd like to do with the Lord's question to Elijah.

The way you mess around with them is to change the emphasis of one word over another.

What was That guy THINKing?!!?   (a rhetorical question)

Becomes "What WAS that guy thinking?" (a real question)

ELIJAH, what are you doing here? (seems like God is angry... but this doesn't fit the context)

Elijah, what are you doing HERE? (as opposed to Bethel or Shiloh or Detroit)

Elijah, what ARE you doing here? [or] Elijah, what are you DOING here? (both helpful questions, but they seem to concern mostly external events)

Most helpful, I think, in terms of our topic of outward zeal, is Elijah, what are YOU doing here?

This invites Elijah to examine himself, his motives, his actions. It invites Elijah to examine his identity.

In my conflict management practice, I often use the mental image of a wood-burning stove.

The top layer is whatever is cooking in the pan... mmm... bacon. You can see, hear, and smell it. But what is making it cook? You have to open up the door. It's the fire underneath.

The fire is the emotion, the feeling, which is making that bacon cook. But most importantly, if you want to understand what's going on, you have to look underneath the flames and see what the fuel is.

What is the wood or the fuel which is making those feelings come up? That's our identity. That's what is at the root of all of our conflicts. Every one of them.

But our identity is also at the root of most of our actions, positive and painful.

There is a woman named Elizabeth, who is the sacristan at my parish. She opens up the church every morning, she turns the lights on and makes sure the linens are ready and the gifts are arranged, and the altar is set, and the books are out, and the candles are lit. Sometimes she's the reader or the altar server or whatever needs to be done. She pampers me, and puts a glass of water out next to my chair every morning Mass. In Arizona, that's a big deal. When I tell her how important she is, and how much I appreciate all that she does, she waves it off and laughingly says "You know what I am, I'm a faithful peon."

What motivates her, in her 80's, to be of such great and reliable service? It is her identity…it's how she sees herself. A faithful peon. Her identity is the fuel that feeds her fire… every morning Mass all week, and on Sundays too. Elizabeth's outward zeal is fed by her inward fire. And her inward fire is fueled by her identity as "a faithful peon". Elizabeth has some sharp edges and at 80-something years old, she has a very gravel-y voice…and some people misjudge her based on those surface things. But I don't. I see the warm, productive fire that gets her up in the morning and over to church. And I see the wood which fuels that warm fire. It is her identity as "a faithful peon" which fuels all the things that she does in our parish.

Now when God asks Elijah "Elijah. What are YOU doing here?", it is an invitation to Elijah to examine himself internally, to examine who he thinks he is… to examine his identity, how he sees himself, and therefore what he actually IS doing there?

And honestly, I don't think the question is entirely a surprise to Elijah. He's been sitting in a cave, after being chased all over Israel by people who want to do him harm, even to kill him. I don't think the question is a surprise, whatever the intonation: "Elijah. What are you doing here?" I'm pretty sure, sitting in his cave, he has asked himself that same question, in every possible pattern. "What AM I doing here?"

And how does Elijah answer this question?

He does not talk about what he owns. "They took away all my stuff!" That's not his answer.

He does not talk about his fame or renown. "They're jealous of me!" That's not his answer.

He does not talk even about what he has done. "I spoke truth to powerful people, and they want to kill me." That's not his answer.

"*Zelo zelatus sum pro domino deo exercituum*" – "I am filled with a jealous zeal for the Lord God of Hosts."

Elijah defines himself by his relationship with God. Elijah defines himself by the God who has filled him.

Zelo Zelatus – What, then, is this zeal? What does it mean?

Zeal has two functions… it works in two ways simultaneously.

Zeal serves as an amplifier, a magnifier, of the emotions we feel on the inside.

Zeal serves as the expression of those emotions

Zeal magnifies (inside phenomenon) and expresses (outside phenomenon) the emotions we feel on the inside

Remember that those feelings (the fire) come from our identity (the fuel)… who we are and how we see ourselves. That's the fuel which feeds our emotions.

So, Zeal then magnifies and expresses the feelings which come from our identity. It magnifies and expresses on the **outside**, whatever is **inside** the person. THAT is why zeal has such a dangerous reputation.

Imagine that I am angry and filled with hatred. I ruminate constantly on my injuries. My primary image of myself, then, is that I am a victim. If I am endlessly aware of the insult, the pain, the injury which I have suffered at the hands of this person, or that person, or this entire group, or even the universe, then my zeal becomes a magnification and an expression of that anger, that hatred.

My zeal becomes something that causes me to fly airplanes into buildings or wrap myself in explosives to detonate in a public place. My zeal becomes something that causes me to drive my car through a crowd of those whom I consider to have harmed me or insulted me.

Maybe my anger and my zeal cause me to do injury even those who just have different perspectives, or values, or skin color, or language, than I do.

My zeal becomes the magnification and expression of my sense of righteous indignation. And righteous indignation is the crack cocaine of our culture. Righteous indignation is an addictive thing, it becomes very easily something that we enjoy, perhaps even seek out. For some, it becomes something they create whenever they can.

It doesn't have to happen just on a scale of global terrorism. Sometimes it happens on the scale of daily life.

When I was in college I worked in a publishing company where I did all kinds of things over the years. On one of these days, one of the tasks I was given was to sort the incoming mail and deliver it to the various people in the offices. At one point, I was delivering mail and came into the employee lunch room and saw a half-dozen employees who seemed to be almost cowering, trapped into a corner by "Tony"... one of the big-shots in the company. He was waving his arms and pointing his finger, and as I walked in, I could hear him finishing off a lecture about how you should NEVER eat a peanut-butter-and-jelly sandwich, because the jelly was so bad for you. Instead, you should ALWAYS make sure it's a peanut-butter-and-preserves sandwich, because preserves were SO much healthier than jelly.

I assumed he was joking, because after all, who would give a lecture to people about peanut-butter-and-jelly sandwiches? As I stood by the door, he turned and said to me, "SNOW! You're a smart guy. What do YOU think? Grape jelly or strawberry preserves?" I thought it would be fun to roll with the joke, so I launched into something like: "Well, whenever you put jelly or preserves on the sandwich, they always soak up into the bread and make it all soggy. So I just have peanut butter sandwiches… they last all day without getting soggy."

"Tony's" response was to say "You're fired." And then he turned back around. I laughed it off and said "OK" and went on my way delivering mail. Later, when I got to the HR office, the woman there said, "I hear 'Tony' fired you." I laughed and put down her mail and said, "Yep. I guess he did." She informed me, "No… he really did fire you. But why don't you take a couple of days off and go on one of those long camping bike-rides of yours, and come back in on Monday. I think we can fix this. But don't let anybody see you here for the next few days."

As it turns out, I got to come back the next Monday and go back to work like before, so whatever this lady, or somebody else, did, it got me my job back. "Tony" was so fragile in his own opinions and values that he had to make sure everybody else agreed with him before he could feel OK about himself. His zeal for healthy eating was really just a magnification and expression of his own fragile self-image, which needed to be propped up and supported by the agreement of everyone else.

Now that's hardly terrorism. But it is mis-directed zeal, based on a damaged sense of identity. It happens on the daily scale like that.

The terrorists and the bomb-makers? They are filled with zeal. But remember that zeal is just a magnification and an expression of what is inside. If you are filled with hate and brooding, then your zeal will be a magnification and expression of that. If you are filled with self-doubt and a fragile opinion of yourself, then your zeal will cause you to fire people over peanut-butter sandwiches.

What if, instead, I am filled with peace?

What if my inner fire is not something which rages and burns out of control, but rather is a steady flame which glows and warms?

What if I am filled with love for God's people, especially that group called the Anawim, the poor, the defenseless, the forgotten, the vulnerable?

What if I am filled with a love of the God who comes to me, as God came to Elijah, not in the earthquake, not in the raging wildfire, but in the gentle, whispering breeze?

What if I have set my soul in God and have learned to recognize God's voice the quiet breath.

What if, indeed, I have learned to recognize and accept the God who comes to me even in the heartache, the struggle, the loss, and the anguish of my life?

What, then would my zeal look like?

Then the steady flame of my zeal, which magnifies and expresses outwardly what lies within, my zeal moves me to tenderly love the Anawim… the ones who are difficult to love.

Then the steady flame of my zeal moves me to act

like my parish's Elizabeth and quietly do all the background work that nobody makes mention of, or even notices… like candles and linens and altar settings and all the other little things which nobody notices until the Elizabeths are gone.

Then the steady flame of my zeal moves me to remember those who are forgotten or who have no one to care for them.

Then the steady flame of my zeal moves me to speak for those who have no voice.

Let me tell you a story about a young man named Mike Meaney. Mike was a kid from my parish in Tucson, Arizona, and later went to our Carmelite high school there called Salpointe. From the time he was very young, Mike had a speech difficulty; he had a stammer. He would get caught on some consonants, and would have to stammer his way through them. He learned some coping techniques and things to make it a little better, but especially when he was young it was a difficult cross to bear. Sometimes junior-high kids can be cruel to those who look or sound different.

In high school, Mike came to me and asked me to be his mentor in a talk he was going to give on a 4-day retreat to his classmates. At that point, Mike had worked his way into everyone's hearts, and was the president of the student body. I told him that "My friends know, don't EVER ask Glenn his opinion unless you really want it." He assured me that he did want my honest opinion. So I read his first draft, and told him, "If you want to give a nice talk that is OK, you can give this talk. It will be OK. But if you want to give a talk that changes people's lives, this one isn't going to cut it. Nowhere in your talk do you even mention the gift of your stammer." Poor Mike was flabbergasted and said, "The GIFT?!!? Do you have ANY idea how much [grief] I have taken for that over the years?!!?" I told him, "I have some idea, yes. But I don't mean it was a gift TO you. That stammer has caused you to really know what it means to be voiceless, to be at the mercy of others who are stronger, or bigger, or just plain louder than you. And look what you have done with it, Mike. You are the president of the school, and you ARE the voice of the students to the faculty and the administration."

Mike graduated from Salpointe and went to Georgetown University, where he also became the president of the student body. A few years later, I was talking with an elderly Jesuit at Creighton, who had spent many years at Georgetown. When I mentioned Salpointe and Tucson, this Jesuit priest asked "Do you know Mike Meaney?" When I told him I did, he told me "He was the best student representative Georgetown ever had. He gave them the voice the student body never had in the hiring committees for new professors."

Yeah. The kid with the stammer became the voice of the voiceless.

Is that not the story of the Passion, Death, and Resurrection of Jesus, written in the lines of our own story? Taking something which is difficult and burdensome for us, and turning it into a gift for someone else? That IS the story of the cross, is it not?

Our zeal is born of our own experience. And our

zeal, like Elijah's, is often (or perhaps always) born of our painful, difficult experiences. Some can brood on that for their entire lives. Some can use that pain… and the result is an anger and a rumination that comes to a boil in destructive actions.

But Elijah, and Jesus, call us to something deeper, something that is indeed God-like. As Elijah did, as Mary did, and as Jesus perfectly did…to take that burden and make it a gift for someone else.

If we allow our difficulties and our burdens to soften, to marinate a while in the love which comes to us from God, then those burdens themselves instead become the steady, warm fire, the zeal, which performs the love of God for the whole world.

In that way, everything is a gift. Everything. Sometimes the gift it TO you. Sometimes the gift is THROUGH you and meant for someone else.

ELIJAH
Inner Fire | Outward Zeal

"Through the gift of ourselves, we undertake to serve, in justice and charity, Jesus himself, who is present in all his brothers and sisters, especially in the little ones and those on the fringes of society. We are to be men and women of service ... in justice and charity." *(Lay Rule #27)*

Lay Carmelites from Louisiana listen to one of the presentations.

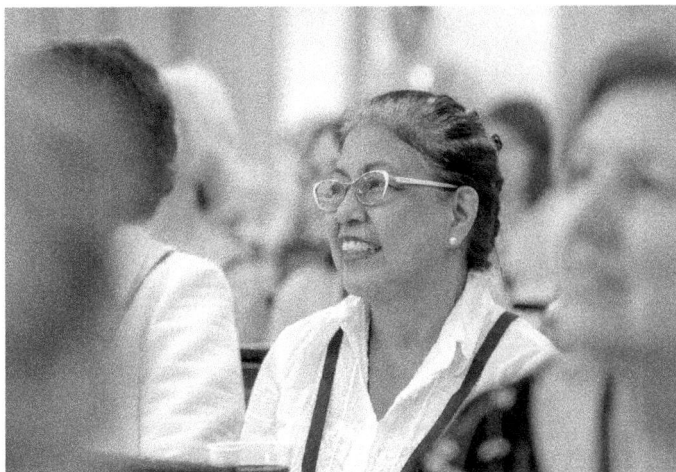

Enrichment and fellowship were the hallmarks of the gathering. Over 350 people attended some part of the Convocation.

William J. Harry, O. Carm.

Fr. William is a native of Louisville, Kentucky and a graduate of the Carmelite high school there. He holds a degree from Marquette University in Teaching History and Philosophy. He also holds a Masters degree from the University of Arizona in Educational Administration. He studied at the Gregorian University in Rome and holds a S.T.B. in Sacred Theology and a S.T.L. in Spirituality. He also holds a D.Min. focused on communications.

He has been involved in secondary education in Carmelite schools as a teacher, campus minister, principal, and school president. He has served as provincial vocation director, editor of provincial publications, commissary provincial, and prior provincial of the Province of the Most Pure Heart of Mary. At the 2001 General Chapter Fr. William was elected General Councilor of the Order, coordinating with the Order in Northern and Central Europe as well as North America (except Mexico). He was also assigned to coordinate the Order's communications, its libraries and archives as well as the Order's institutes of scientific research around the world.

He is currently the director of communications for the Order as well as director of the book publications department of Carmelite Media and editor of *The Sword* magazine. He lives and works in the province's formation house for professed students in Huizucar, El Salvador.

THE CALL OF ELIJAH IS OUR CALL-

presented by William J. Harry, O. Carm.

So let's talk a bit about "calls" from God. The prophets began their prophetic careers as the result of a definite call. The true prophets entered the prophetic ministry because of the constraint of God's will. They are not acting on their own but because of an encounter (had a dream, heard a voice, etc.) with God. They each have their own story:

Amos, the herdsman from Tekoa, declared that he prophesied not out of personal choice, but because God took him from following the flock and inducted him into the prophetic ministry (Amos 7:14-15).

Hosea, the brokenhearted husband, saw in his tragic domestic experience the heartbreak of God and felt constrained to proclaim the suffering love of Israel's Maker (Hos. 1-3).

Isaiah, the aristocrat, heard the voice of the divine Sovereign calling for a messenger and knew that the call was meant for him (Isa. 6).

Micah felt that he was possessed by his message and the power to deliver it (Mic. 3:8).

Jeremiah, the shy and sheltered youth, found himself conscripted into a position from which his timid nature caused him to shrink (Jer. 1:6).

> The words of Jeremiah son of Hilkiah, one of the priests at Anathoth in the territory of Benjamin. The word of the Lord came to him in the thirteenth year of the reign of Josiah son of Amon king of Judah, and through the reign of Jehoiakim son of Josiah king of Judah, down to the fifth month of the eleventh year of Zedekiah son of Josiah king of Judah, when the people of Jerusalem went into exile.

Hmm. Pretty specific when this happened. And what was said to him: "The word of the Lord came to me, saying, 'Before I formed you in the womb I knew you …'"

Ezekiel was set as a watchman over Israel in order that he might warn them to turn from their wicked ways (Ezek. 2:8 f).

We have the same with Isaiah: Chapter 1 verses 1-2:

> The vision concerning Judah and Jerusalem that Isaiah son of Amoz saw during the reigns of Uzziah, Jotham, Ahaz and Hezekiah, kings of Judah. Hear me, you heavens! Listen, earth! For the LORD has spoken.

These folks were very aware of God's summoning and sustaining them as they became God's agents to reveal his message to the people. "This experience" of the soul's confrontation with the living God "is central and determinative" of all that is to follow in their lives. Everything they did was shaped by this initial call.

What about your own call? If you had to come up

here and talk about your "call" this morning, what you say? How accepting of the call have you been? What do you believe your call has actually asked you to do?

It would be helpful to see just what God said to Elijah when he called him! And here we have a bit of a problem. We do not have a detailed, clear-cut initial call from God. We do not have actual words. Nor do we have a specific action. We are picking up the story already in progress. When we arrive at Chapter 17 of the First Book of Kings, we find Elijah is already on scene and at work being the prophet. He is confronting King Ahab—

> Now Elijah the Tishbite, from Tishbe in Gilead, said to Ahab, "As the Lord, the God of Israel, lives, whom I serve, there will be neither dew nor rain in the next few years except at my word.

What? This Elijah character is telling the king that he is going to control the rains over the next few years? What on earth brought this about? Well ... if you go back to Chapter 16, it finishes with "King Ahab did more to provoke the LORD God of Israel to anger than all the kings of Israel that were before him." Ahab is actually a minor king. Yet he is one of the best remembered. Why? Because he "did more to provoke Yahweh that any other king of Israel before him." So we already suspect he is going to get smacked by Yahweh in some way. Chapter 16 ends. Chapter 17 begins. "Elijah, the Tishbite" is already on scene to deal with King Ahab! Elijah has already received his call and is responding with 120% effort. He confronts King Ahab:

> As the Lord, the God of Israel, lives, whom I serve,
> there will be neither dew nor rain in the next few
> years except at my word.

That is pretty gutsy— telling the King that I am going to control that water in your kingdom and there is nothing you can do about it!! But that is what Elijah understood God wanted him to do and say! And as we see, this initial "call" of God to his prophet is "central and determinative" of all that is to follow in Elijah's life. It is not that Elijah was always happy about what he was told to do. Nor did he always feel up to the task. Elijah, at one point, felt so overwhelmed by what God was telling him to do that he just sat down and said "I have had it. Take my life." (More about that later!)

Fr. Kilian Healy in his book *Prophet of Fire* points out the difference between the Hebrew and the Vulgate translation of this text. The Hebrew text:

> As the Lord, the God of Israel, lives, **whom I serve**,
> there will be neither dew nor rain in the next few
> years except at my word.

The Vulgate which Fr. Kilian points out had great influence on Carmelite tradition, emphasized Elijah being in God's presence. Instead of "whom I serve" the translation was "before whom I stand" So the text read "as the Lord the God of Israel live, before whom I stand, there shall be neither dew nor rain these years, except by my word."

Personally I like either translation: "before whom I stand" and "whom I serve." Or better, I prefer both of these translations together. For me, it is important to have both "before whom I stand" and "whom I serve" as they capture these two essential elements of Carmelite life that I think we probably all struggle with– finding a balance between "standing" (contemplation) and "serving" (ministry/active life). I do not believe it makes any difference if you live in a cloistered monastery or if you are the parent of six children. Finding the proper balance between "standing" and "serving," will be a struggle.

BE OPEN TO TRANSFORMATION!

In Darien where we have a very active retreat house, one of the summer offerings is a week's retreat on various aspects of Carmelite life. This is the second year they have run it. I just got home from Peru on Thursday night/Friday morning so I went over for breakfast to see everyone. (I am VERY Elian. I let others fix me food!) For a portion of the breakfast, I sat with the Carmelite nuns from Wahpeton, North Dakota as I have not seen them in a couple of years and it has not been their practice to participate in such meetings. But they have a very dynamic prioress and there they all were. One of the cloistered nuns said to me, "It has been a VERY good week. I have so much to think about. This week has been very challenging. So, I have to go home and think about all this and how it applies to me."

I told her she was going to be a part of my talk today and she thought that was great. But it really struck me that a cloistered Carmelite nun (who has been around the cloister walk a few times--- that is a religious way of saying "she is not so young") would be so open to new ideas and allowing her structures which were built over a number of years to be challenged. It surprised me a bit that she would be open to a "transformation" in her spiritual life. But I think it is exactly what is supposed to happen!

Transformation seems to be an often forgotten part of Elijah's call. Elijah was often having to physically change from where he is at the moment to another geographical location because God was calling him to go to a new place.

He is a Tishbite but he is not in his homeland when we meet him. He has already left his home in order to answer God's call and be a prophet of God.

Then the word of the Lord came to him: "Go at once to Zarephath in the region of Sidon and stay there."

The Lord said to him, "Go back the way you came, and go to the Desert of Damascus."

Of course, in there instances we are talking about a geographic location change. God tells Elijah to go to Zarephath. God tells Elijah to go to the Desert of Damascus. But I understand this as a call for an interior or moral change as well. I understand it as a call to move from one's pre-conceived notions as well— move to an area where these are less rigid, more open to be able to be penetrated by the grace of our God. Of course, it could be a major challenge to move from our tightly held beliefs to a new place where we are then willing to take an honest look at new ideas, changing ideas. That is what transformation is all about. That Carmelite nun was telling me the same– "Gee, I thought I was doing so well and now I have been challenged to sharpen what it is I believe and how I am supposed to live my beliefs out."

But we are always changing, new circumstances are coming at us, new situations arise constantly, and our spiritual understanding needs to evolve (maybe not the best word to use here!). Otherwise we are living out an immature faith, a faith that has not been been nourished, tested, or even dusted off.

Elijah, in the midst of his anxiety, learned to his surprise, that God's cause did not depend on him. Quite the contrary, he learned his prophetic task was totally dependent on God. It is God who defends Elijah, not Elijah who must defend God!

Elijah had to be open to a transformation of consciousness. He had to adjust his old vision to a new reality. He had to be open to conversion. Even in his old age and supported by his many victories in God's cause, he was not ashamed to open himself up to a new and more transforming experience of his God, ever new and ever full of surprise. Elijah had to learn that God was not with him only in his victories, but also in his depression, anguish, and flight.

Following Christ is not for the faint hearted. It is tough work. I spend time trying to respond to my vocational call and then someone comes up and challenges me to look at things differently. And suddenly I realized that just because I "do" what I think is required of me, I am not a holy person. I am a person who goes through the motions but not always with my heart involved. In fact, I can be difficult to live with or be with. (Of course, I am speaking hypothetically here!)

You know, I think if we genuinely believe in a God who is love, that should make us smile. It should make us a joyful people. It should make us warm and friendly. But I can tell you a lot of us missed that boat when it sailed. Some of us who spend lots of time talking about prayer (and generally how others are not doing it or not doing it correctly) are some of the angriest people around. I told one of them "If that is what prayer is doing for you, I think I will be doing less praying!" Others act like they are carrying the weight of the world on their shoulders. I was having dinner at an outdoor café by the Vatican one evening and every member of the clergy who passed us, sporting their collars and blacksuits, and the standard black briefcases, looked like their puppy had just died. There was no look of joy— let alone any Pascal joy!!! I felt sorry for them. Apparently they could not even be happy that they were finally leaving work for the day! Granted not every day as a Christian is going to be joyful. There is the element of the Cross in the life of every Christian. But after the Cross comes the Resurrection and we would do well to focus more energy on that aspect of our Christian life.

WRESTLE WITH GOD!

Oh no. You want us to wrestle with God? I cannot do that, you might be thinking. He is God. I am just me. If that is what is going through you head, I say "Nonsense!" You should wrestle with God once in a while. Don't you ever get mad about something involving God? Don't you wish he had selected someone else to endure what you are enduring? Don't you think God is very unfair sometimes? Don't you think he plays favorites and you have the feeling that you are not one of them? You should be a favorite! After all, you are a Lay Carmelite! You are a good person. Yet the fellow next door that won the $500 million lottery is not every a nice person!!! So you never get upset with God?

What does this have to do with Elijah? Fr. Glenn talked about the Carmelite motto *Zelo zelatus sum, pro Domino Deum Exercituum.* It is what Elijah said to Yahweh just after he encounters God in the gentle breeze. A voice says to Elijah, "What are you doing here, Elijah?"

And Elijah responds, "I am filled with zealous zeal for the Lord God of Hosts." Let me give you my translation of what Elijah is really saying. Is he really saying, "Oh God. I am totally yours"? I think not. Right after saying that, Elijah says, "The Israelites have rejected your covenant, torn down your altars, and put your prophets to death with the sword. I am the only one left, and now they are trying to kill me too."

Elijah is ticked off. He is mad. He is beside himself actually. He is fearful for his life. "I have remained faithful to you. I have not only done what you required but I have done it with great zeal. And what have you done in this bargain? Your people rejected your covenant, they torn down your altars, they killed your prophets. I am the only one and they are going to kill me. Thanks a lot for hanging me out to dry." (Somehow, I think Elijah's language would be much stronger!)

We have got to get over this idea that we cannot speak frankly with God. If I am angry with my best friend, I will tell them. Otherwise, the anger stays inside of me. It may be tamped down. But it will squeeze out somewhere, sometime. And then that anger tends to be worse because it was allowed to fester. And if my relationship with my friends is based on mutual trust, understanding, and forgiveness, do I not have to speak honestly with them? A relationship that cannot withstand honesty is not much of a healthy, loving relationship.

The same is true in our relationships with God. Wrestle with God! Be genuine with God! If you want to scream at him, go ahead and scream at him. Trust me. He can handle it. Maintain a healthy, loving relationship with your loving God!!! (And why not! Remember God already knows what you are thinking and feeling! It isn't like you are fooling him by not being honest!)

I had a very powerful experience of this at a parish I was administering for a few months in Tucson, Arizona. The Sunday reading was about St. Thomas the Apostle who is more commonly known as "Doubting Thomas." The parish is dedicated to St. Thomas the Apostle. In the Gospel story, Thomas required additional proof of the Resurrected Christ. And the Lord gives that proof to him and Thomas comes to full faith. So I said to the parishioners (and I often say to our Carmelite students), "Don't be afraid of doubts. Embrace them. They are a gift from God. They can purify your faith. They can help you come to understand with clarity and conviction what it is you believe and why you believe it." I said "We are St. Thomas the Apostle Parish—named after someone who had actually walked the Earth with Our Lord and still he needed more proof to overcome his doubts. As members of this parish dedicated to Doubting Thomas, we should be experts in doubting!"

After Mass an elderly man came up to me and he was crying. He said "I have had doubts all my life. I have prayed to God that he would take these doubts away. But he never did. I would get so angry. But I never thought I could express my anger to God. You are the first person who ever said to me that it is okay to have doubts! And now I realize that if I had expressed my anger over my doubts, I might be a man of stronger faith today."

Don't be afraid of having a very frank conversation with God. Wrestle with God. You are not going to say anything he does not already know.

WHAT THE "LAY CARMELITE RULE" SAYS ABOUT ELIJAH

Allow me to make a few introductory comments. I was on the General Council when we approved this so-called Rule. I was against its title actually. You are Carmelites. You have a Rule, the *formula vitae* handed on by Albert of Jerusalem! That Rule was actually written for the lay people on Mount Carmel! You cannot have two Rules! And there is something fishy to me about a Rule that is changed every few years. For me a Rule is the foundational document of an Order and sets out primary values to be held in the Order. That is NOT what this document is. It is really the Constitutions of the Lay Carmelites, like the Carmelites who are priests and brothers have our own Constitutions. The Carmelite nuns have their own Constitutions. But we all follow the one Rule of St. Albert. These introductory comments have nothing to do with this talk on Elijah. But I take every opportunity I can to clarify what I think is a very unfortunate treatment of Lay Carmelites.

So since this document—just approved in the first decade of this century—is directed at the Lay Carmelites and their vocation, does what does the document say about Elijah?

Number 26 does not mention Elijah by name but speaks of the prophetic office of Christ and the Church … assimilating the Gospel through faith and to proclaim it by their works. This commitment includes not hesitating to denounce even courageously. Many other places in the document contain similar mention of "activities" which Lay Carmelites are supposed to undertake: service of God's kingdom, for example in number 27 ("Through the gift of ourselves, we undertake to serve, in justice and charity, Jesus himself, who is present in all his brothers and sisters, especially in the little ones and those on the fringes of society. We are to be men and women of service … in justice and charity.")

We could read through most of the paragraphs and pull out what the Rule of the Lay Carmelites calls you to do which is certainly based on Elijah being one of the two inspirations of the Order. (The other being Mary, of course.)

Number 35 is clearest. "Lay Carmelites also share the zeal of the prophet Elijah for the Lord and his law. They are ready to defend the rights of those who are downtrodden. They learn from the prophet to leave everything to go into the desert in order to be purified, made ready for their meeting with the Lord and to welcome his word. They feel impelled, like the prophet, to support true religion against false idols."

"Together with Elijah, Lay Carmelites learn to feel the presence of the Lord which comes to humanity with strength and gentleness. He is the same yesterday, today, and forever. Strengthened by this transforming and life-giving experience, lay Carmelites are able to face the realities of the world, confident that God holds the destiny of each one and the whole of history itself." Then it cites 1 Kgs 17-19.

Number 47 begins by talking about St. Mary Magdalene de Pazzi and the redemption of souls through a union of prayer and apostolate. It then says this: "Lay Carmelites, ready to witness to their faith by their works, receive the strength to draw people to God … In times of loss and change, they can give many people reliable direction. So too the prophet Elijah was caught up in a world of great change and which led many people to abandon the true God. They thought they were self-sufficient. Elijah was sustained by his certainty that God was stronger than any crisis or any danger. So Lay Carmelites live in a world which is ever more uncertain in the face of fundamental questions, and in an era which has presented new problems for faith, morals, and society. They strive to create opportunities for proclaiming Christ."

I spoke yesterday in my homily at Mass about our response as Carmelites to situations in the world.

I was speaking yesterday from the point of view of community discernment. I wanted to stress that we as a group should be discerning how we must confront situations that have arisen in our world.

Today I would say it is clear in your own Rule, in number #47. "It is clear that we must look for opportunities to proclaim Christ. To denounce unjust situations. To defend the rights of the downtrodden. We know we cannot sit idlily by." Being a follower of Christ is not a spectator sport. We are compelled to get involved. It is who we are. It is what we are. It stems directly from Elijah in Scripture as an inspiration of our Order.

There is much that could be expanded on in each point that I touched on. But that is for us to work on over the years: how to truly live the inspiration of Elijah, each within our own vocational call. Our lives as Carmelites need to confirm with our lives that Elijah's Call and his response is our call as well. May our response be as firm in faith.

Kathleen Richardville, TOC, poses with Fr. Fernando Millán Romeral and his presentation copy of the song *Fernando*. Kathleen wrote the lyrics using the melody of the ABBA song *Fernando*. It was performed by the entire assembly during the banquet in recognition the prior general's 12 years of service to the Order on the occasion of his last official trip to the USA.

Musical Gift from the Lay Carmelites of North America to Fernando Millán Romeral, O. Carm.

on the occasion of his last trip to the USA as prior general

We are here today, Fernando,

As one fam'ly zealous in the love of God.

And we welcome you Fernando,

Once again your presence graces and inspires us anew.

You have travelled many lands

As pilgim, leader, touching countless hearts and hands.

Did you ever think, Fernando,

As a boy in Spain so many year long past,

That a still small voice would lead you

As a writer, teacher, priest, and leader of our family vast?

And you've served us very well

In more way than we have time or words to tell.

Refrain

There was Something from above, those days,

To guide your ways, Fernando.

It was always in your words, your grace,

Your smiling face, Fernando

And you love of God so true,

And his love for you ...

It was just as it was meant to be

Eternally, Fernando.

As you surely know, Fernando,

A leader's mantle weighs one down in joy and pain,

And you may have wished, Fernando,

Many times to go back to your former life again,

When the challenges ran deep,

And earnest prayer prevented you from sleep.

In your role as Prior General

You ahve been a humble servant from the start.

In the footsteps of the Master,

With His joy, His grace and love poured from your heart,

Wearing Mary's habit true,

Caring for the Carmelites who now thank you.

Refrain

Do you hear applause, Fernando?

Do you see our joy, our tears, our feelings true?

Do you hear our song, Fernando?

Do you know the silent prayers we lift for you,

In this special time of praise

To strengthen you through all the coming days?

Final Refrain

There is something in the room today

From Carmelites, Fernando.

Its a love for everyone to share,

Grace everywhere, Fernando.

And to show that it's all true

We say to you ...

If you could lead us forth, again,

We'd say "Amen" Fernando.

Yes, if you could lead us forth, again,

We'd say "Amen" Fernando!

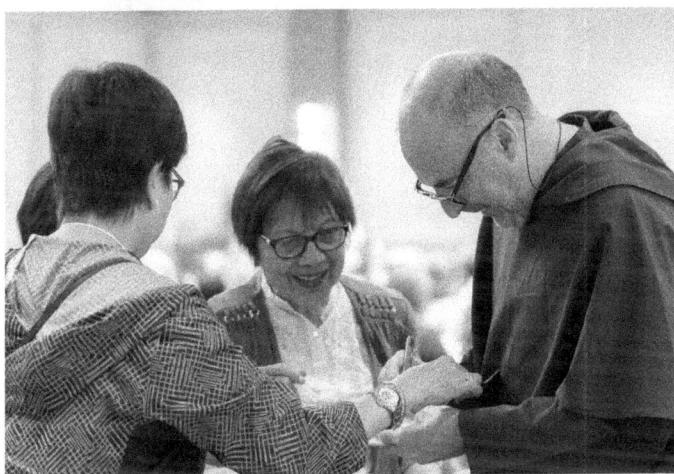

(Above) Fr. Fernando captures his own video of the Lay Carmelites singing an adaptation of *Fernando* in his honor during the banquet. (Below) Fr. Fernando signs copies of the song *Fernando* following its debut at the 2019 Lay Carmelite Convocation. It was just one of the moments when the Lay Carmelites showed appreciation for Fr. Fernando's service to the Order over the last 12 years.

RECOMMENDED CARMELITE WEBSITES

For more information about the Carmelites today,
our spirituality and our ministries worldwide, visit:

The Carmelite Order: ocarm.org

The Most Pure Heart of Mary Province: carmelites.net

Center for Carmelite Studies at Catholic University of America:

carmelites.info/CenterForCarmeliteStudies

Carmelite Institute of North America:
carmeliteinstitute.net

Instituto de las Americas:
institutocarmelitano.carmelitas.org

For a listing of Carmelite provinces worldwide, visit:
carmelites.info/provinces

For a listing of Monasteries of Carmelite nuns, visit:
carmelites.info/nuns

For a listing of Carmelite Hermitages, please visit:
carmelites.info/hermits

For a listing of sites about Lay Carmelites:
carmelites.info/lay carmel

For a listing of Affiliated Congregations and Institutes:
carmelites.info/congregations

For our work with the United Nations, visit:
carmelitengo.org

For more information about publications, visit:
carmelites.info/publications